The Fastest Way to Create and Grow Your Family Tree

123 Family Tree

ancestrypublishing

The Library of Congress has cataloged the third edition as follows:

1-2-3 family tree : the fastest way to create and grow your family tree ancestry. — 3rd ed.
    p. cm.
Includes bibliographical reference and index.
ISBN 1-59331-296-2 (softcover : alk. paper)
 1. Genealogy. 2. United States--Genealogy--Handbooks, manuals, etc. I. Title:
One, two, three family tree.

CS16 .A15 2006c
929'.1'072073—dc22

2006016590

First edition 2001
Second edition 2002
Third edition 2006
Fourth edition 2007

10 9 8 7 6 5 4 3 2 1
ISBN-13: 978-1-59331-312-8
ISBN-10: 1-59331-312-8

Printed in the United Sates of America.

Table of Contents

Introduction

Welcome to the *1-2-3 Family Tree* guidebook. You are about to embark on an adventure—one that is exciting, rewarding, and easier than ever with the help of modern-day advances such as computers and the Internet. The three simple steps of *1-2-3 Family Tree* will get you well on your way to discovering your family tree:

- **Step One** will help you gather and analyze the information you already know about yourself and your family. And by using a few simple techniques to gather more information, you will learn to fill in the gaps.

- **Step Two** will show you how to organize your information with the easy-to-use *Family Tree Maker* software.

- **Step Three** will help you broaden your search in a variety of ways to find more information about your family.

With the information and research tools you'll find in this guide, you will be able to create a personal family tree that will help you better understand yourself and your family.

Are you ready? Let's begin!

Step One

Gather Information About Your Family

In Step One you will:

- Start with yourself. Then list all the names of your parents, grandparents, and great-grandparents that you know, as well as their birth, marriage, and death information where possible.

- Learn what home sources are available to you and what they can tell you about your family.

- Learn how to conduct an effective interview.

Sandy Gets Started

Sandy Sorenson hadn't anticipated getting involved in family history research until the day her mother decided her house was just too big to keep up. Sandy's mother asked for her help in sorting and packing up the household in preparation for her move into a condo. Sandy's children were both in college, and Sandy was thinking that a condo might also be in her future. She was so absorbed in her thoughts that she almost tossed out an old box of papers and books before she saw her father's name. Her father had died a few years before, and since then, Sandy had been thinking how little she had known about him.

Looking through the box, she saw some letters from her father's parents, apparently written to him while he was at college. Reading through the letters, she learned that her father was the first person in his family to attend college. She also realized that her grandfather was originally from Michigan. She'd always assumed he had been born in their home state of California.

Realizing that she knew almost nothing about her father's family, Sandy asked her mother to tell her about her father and his family. Then, while she was writing down names, Sandy decided to ask about her mother's family as well. Although at first her mother was reluctant to talk about the past, she was soon telling stories about various members of the family as Sandy scribbled down notes and asked questions.

At home that evening, Sandy looked over her notes. Her mother wasn't sure of some names and she couldn't remember any dates, but at least Sandy knew more now than she'd known before. She decided to write a few letters to some relatives and introduce herself. For some reason

Get Started

How do you get started with your family tree? Write down everything you already know about yourself, your parents, and your grandparents. Don't worry if you don't know much. Get it down on paper first.

she couldn't explain, she felt an urgent need to learn all she could about her ancestors and where her family had come from.

Begin with You

At some point in life, people feel compelled to learn more about the individuals in their family who came before them. Genealogy is the study of our ancestors and their lives—where they were born, where they lived, where they died. Family history is taking that information and filling in the blanks with the many events that made up their lives. Using newspapers, military records, etc., we are able to discover the stories of their lives.

What makes genealogy and family history research even more interesting is seeing the impact that our ancestors' lives had on our own lives. They may have had many children or a few, settled in a large city or on a farm, or relocated frequently or stayed in the same area for generations. Their decisions in some way have affected our lives.

A few lucky individuals may have a family Bible full of names and dates or perhaps an ancestor's journal or life history, but most people have to dig around a bit to find who their ancestors were, where they lived, even where they came from. You will want to lay some groundwork before beginning to research an ancestor who emigrated from another country many years ago. This is why, in researching your family and ancestors, you will want to start with yourself and your immediate family.

Take a few minutes right now using Worksheet A to list your birth date and place as well as any other dates of significance in your life (e.g., religious events, education, marriage, etc.).

Genealogy Jargon

Given Name First and middle names.

Surname, Family, or Birth Name Last name at birth.

Maiden Name The surname of a woman before she marries.

Tips of the Trade

When filling out the worksheets in this chapter, it is helpful to follow a few standard family history practices:

Whenever you can, use full names. Be sure to include middle names, nicknames (in quotation marks), suffixes (Jr., Esq.), maiden names, and relevant titles (Rev., Capt., Dr.).

Record surnames in all caps. With some names, it can be easy to misinterpret which name is the surname and which is the given name. Otherwise, Charles David could easily be read David Charles.

List females by birth or maiden names, not married names. If you only know your ances-tor's married name, include it, but enclose it in parentheses like this: Mary (Jones).

Include as much information as you can about each location. Standard format includes city, county/parish, and state/province/country. Two-letter state abbreviations are preferable.

As you add dates, use the international method of date entry. List the day first, the standard three-letter abbreviation of the month, and then all four digits of the year. For example, October 11, 1884 should be written 11 Oct 1884 instead of 10/11/1884 so it will never be misinterpreted as 10 Nov 1884.

YOUR FULL NAME _Sandra "Sandy" WARNER_

BIRTH Date | **Place**
23 Sep 1940 | Santa Rosa, Sonoma, CA

RELIGIOUS EVENTS

Event	Date	Place
Baptism / Christening		St. Rose
First Communion	May 1948	St. Rose

EDUCATION

	Date	Place
High School graduation	1958	Ursuline High School
College diploma	Jun 1978	Santa Clara University

MARRIAGE

Spouse	Date	Place
David Gary SORENSON	6 Jun 1959	Santa Rosa, Sonoma, CA

Sandy's partially completed Worksheet A

WORKSHEET A: Your Vital Information

YOUR FULL NAME _____

BIRTH Date   **Place**

RELIGIOUS EVENTS

Event	Date	Place

EDUCATION	Date	Place

MARRIAGE

Spouse	Date	Place

CHILDREN

Name	Date	Place

WORKSHEET B: Your Parents' Vital Information

YOUR FATHER'S FULL NAME _____

BIRTH Date | Place
| |

DEATH Date | Place
| |

YOUR MOTHER'S FULL NAME _____
(first name and maiden name)

BIRTH Date | Place
| |

DEATH Date | Place
| |

MARRIAGE Date | Place
| |

CHILDREN

Name	Date	Place

OTHER SIGNIFICANT EVENTS

Event	Date	Place

When you have filled out as much as you can, move on to Worksheet B and list the same information for your parents. You may need to leave some spaces blank. That's okay. You'll be able to fill them in later.

If you know information about your grandparents, fill it in next using Worksheets C and D, which ask for information about your father's parents and your mother's parents. Again, don't worry about any spaces you can't fill in. You can also telephone your parents to see if they can help you fill in the gaps. Later on, you can conduct a more thorough interview, but a quick phone call can save you a lot of time at this point.

Sandy Finds Buried Treasures

While speaking with her mother-in-law one day, Sandy mentioned her new interest in genealogy. Although Sandy's husband, Gary, was only mildly interested in what Sandy was doing, he had told her everything he knew about his family.

"You don't happen to have an old family Bible, do you?" she asked her mother-in-law. "You know, with names and dates written on the inside jacket."

The older woman shook her head. She did, however, have a few boxes of family stuff in the attic. She dreaded having to sort through them and admitted that she was ready to just throw them out since she'd never needed anything in them.

Sandy volunteered to sort through the boxes and spent several rewarding hours examining their contents.

WORKSHEET C: Your Paternal Grandparents' Vital Information

NAME OF FATHER'S FATHER _____

BIRTH Date | Place

DEATH Date | Place

NAME OF FATHER'S MOTHER _____
(first name and maiden name)

BIRTH Date | Place

DEATH Date | Place

MARRIAGE Date | Place

CHILDREN

Name	Date	Place

OTHER SIGNIFICANT EVENTS

Event	Date	Place

WORKSHEET D: Your Maternal Grandparents' Vital Information

NAME OF MOTHER'S FATHER_____

BIRTH Date | Place
[   ] [   ]

DEATH Date | Place
[   ] [   ]

NAME OF MOTHER'S MOTHER _____
(first name and maiden name)

BIRTH Date | Place
[   ] [   ]

DEATH Date | Place
[   ] [   ]

MARRIAGE Date | Place
[   ] [   ]

CHILDREN

Name	Date	Place

OTHER SIGNIFICANT EVENTS

Event	Date	Place

More than 16 million immigrants entered the United States through Ellis Island

She found some old property deeds, newspaper clippings of interest to the family, military discharge papers, and of course, pictures. She laughed when she discovered her father-in-law's high school report cards. They didn't give her any genealogical information, but they did offer some insight into his personality as a young man.

Perhaps the most exciting discovery she made was her husband's grandfather's will. It gave the names of his wife and children, as well as the location of his home and property. It also named two more people in a preceding generation.

Sandy was startled by the contents of the second box, which held, among other things, an application for naturalization for Gary's great-grandfather, with his full name, year of immigration, country of origin, and more. Perhaps he had even come through Ellis Island, she mused.

Home Sources

Bibles	Memoirs
Books (check inscriptions)	Newspaper clippings
Certificates	Notebooks
Church memorabilia	Oral histories
Diaries	Passports
Drivers' licenses	Postcards
Employment documents	Photograph albums
Estate papers	Religious items
Funeral cards	Report cards
Genealogies (from relatives)	School publications
Graduation memorabilia	Scrapbooks
Histories (for family, town, etc.)	Tax records
Immigration papers	Uniforms
Insurance papers	Vaccination records
Jewelry	Voter registration
Journals	War memorabilia
Land records	Wedding announcements
Letters	Wills
Medical records	Yearbooks

She also found a journal, and although half the pages were blank and the writing was faded, Sandy could hardly wait to read through it.

Check Out Your Attic

If you've been feeling discouraged about the blank spaces in your family tree, don't be! You'll soon learn lots of ways to help you fill in those blanks.

For now, consider the sources you have in your own home. Many people don't realize that their home may hold valuable information about their family. For instance, you may have letters from your parents or even grandparents or other relatives that contain information about the family. Or perhaps you have certificates of accomplishment for family members. School report cards, programs, even announcements, all give clues about personalities as well as dates of events.

Perhaps it's time to take a weekend vacation to visit your parents. You may even decide to call on an elderly aunt or uncle you've been meaning to visit anyway. While visiting, ask about letters, scrapbooks, military memorabilia, school records, licenses, and keepsakes.

Ask your parents and brothers and sisters to check their attics as well. You might just rescue a critical piece of information they did not know they had hidden away in an old box of papers.

Keep a Record of Your Sources

As you begin to record the information you have gathered on your lists, remember to note where the information came from. Whether your source is a conversation with a family member, a family Bible, a treasured letter, a birth certificate, or a published family history, you'll want to keep a clear record of your sources. Even if you learned the information from a quick telephone conversation, record who gave you the information and when.

For example, what if sometime down the road you decide you want to go back and examine the document or item more carefully. Would you be able to retrace your steps?

Genealogy Jargon

Research Log A written record detailing your research progress.

What if another family member wanted to analyze the source as well? Using only the source information you have given, could someone else find the same information?

What if another family member, inspired by your findings, decided to write a book about your family and your ancestors? Your list of sources would provide the basis for a bibliography. Would the sources be easy to find?

What if you or another member of your family decided to apply for membership in a family organization, such as the Daughters of the American Revolution (DAR)? You will be asked to document your lineage.

The *Family Tree Maker* (*FTM*) software included with this book has a specific place to record source information. You will learn more about this software in the following step. While many people enjoy this feature, for now it may be more convenient to use Worksheet E, the Research Log. Another option is to record information about the individuals in your family tree on separate 3" x 5" cards, using each

WORKSHEET E: Research Log

Family _____   Researcher _____

Date	Repository Call #/Microfilm #	Description of Source	Time Period/ Names Searched	Results

WORKSHEET F: Contact List for Living Sources

NAME

Address

Phone | Fax | E-mail

Date of Visit | Date Letter Sent | Date Received Reply

Notes

––––––––––––––––––––––––––––––––––––

NAME

Address

Phone | Fax | E-mail

Date of Visit | Date Letter Sent | Date Received Reply

Notes

––––––––––––––––––––––––––––––––––––

NAME

Address

Phone | Fax | E-mail

Date of Visit | Date Letter Sent | Date Received Reply

Notes

card to represent a new person. Write the name of each ancestor at the top and use the rest of the card to list whatever information you find. Then use the back of the card to record the source of your information.

Ask Relatives and Family Members

The two basic methods of collecting information from living sources are personal interviewing and letter writing. Use both of these methods to gather your information.

First, use Worksheet F to list the people in your family you could contact. Look over the names on your list and indicate which individuals you would feel comfortable visiting and speaking with. For family members who live some distance away or who you may not know very well, you may prefer to write to them. (Old Christmas card lists or a wedding register may be helpful in locating addresses of relatives.)

Interview Your Relatives

Take time before conducting an interview to make sure you are prepared with the questions you want to ask. Use the interview questions provided on page 16 to stimulate your relatives' memories and conversation. Remember that you are trying to gather as much information as possible so keep the memories flowing. There is no need to rush to the next question. Most people don't remember precise dates for the events in their family, but they do remember stories. Just let them talk. You will need to research dates later by contacting

Interview Questions

Childhood

Where did you live as a child?

What are your most vivid childhood memories?

What are your favorite memories of your grandparents?

Tell me about the most serious illness you had as a child.

Which of your neighbors were most memorable?

What do you remember about your childhood friends and the people in your neighborhood?

Family

What do you remember best about your mother?

What do you remember best about your father?

How are you like your parents? How are you unlike your parents?

What do you remember best about your brothers and sisters?

In what ways did your parents/siblings influence your growing-up years?

What do you remember about things you did with parents/siblings?

Was religion important in your home? If so, what practices made it important?

Did you have a favorite uncle or aunt? What do you best remember about him or her?

What were your family traditions?

What holidays were special in your family? What did you do to celebrate them?

School and Friends

What do you remember best about your grade school years?

What do you remember best about junior high and high school?

What subjects and activities did you enjoy most? Least?

What kinds of things did you and your friends enjoy doing together?

Tell me about your first romance.

What things do you enjoy doing today that you also enjoyed in your youth?

What do you remember about being a teenager? What was important to you then? What were your dreams and goals?

Education and Career

Was higher education important to you? If so, what educational experiences were pivotal in your life?

How did you decide what to study?

What do you remember about your first job?

How much did you make and how did you spend your money?

How did you choose your vocation and how have you liked it?

How many jobs have you had? Which did you like most? Least?

Describe your work duties, the work environment, what you learned.

Marriage and Parenthood

How did you meet your spouse?

What made you decide to marry your spouse?

How did parenthood change you? Tell me about your children.

What events most changed your life?

Current Events

Who was the president of the United States while you were in high school?

What events were people talking about while you were growing up? (e.g., wars, inventions, etc.)

When did you first become interested in the world outside of your family and friends?

What were the defining events of your life?

vital records offices, looking through old newspapers, searching court records, etc.

Explain the purpose of the interview to the individual with whom you are speaking. Take careful notes and bring a tape recorder or video camera as well. Be sure to ask permission to record the interview, but don't let the equipment get in the way of a good interview.

Photo Clues

Examine those old photographs carefully. Clothing can provide clues to help you discover the origins of your family and date the photograph.

Photographs can be very useful in prompting memories. If you have any old photographs, take them along to the interview. They can provide a powerful "trigger" to bring old memories to the surface. Even if you can't identify the people in an old photograph, ask about them during the interview. The answers you find may open new avenues for exploration into your family tree.

When you have completed an interview, be sure to write down the date and place of the interview as well as the name of the individual you interviewed. That is the source for this information. (As noted earlier, there is a place to record this information in your *Family Tree Maker* software as well.)

Interviews

You will obtain good family information from your relatives by asking open-ended questions: Who were you named for? What stories did your grandmother tell you? Where did you go to school? What was your favorite holiday? Tell me about your military service.

When you return home, take time to (1) look through your notes, using a marker to highlight key points and any names, dates, or events that may have been mentioned, (2) clarify and expand anything that is hard to read or confusing in your notes, and (3) transcribe the recorded tape so you have a complete and accessible copy of the information you gained in your interview. Otherwise, you could lose this valuable information if the tape is lost or damaged or accidentally taped over.

Write Letters

For those people who live some distance away, write a brief letter or e-mail of introduction and explain your interest in the information you are seeking. Keep your letter short (there will be time for lengthy, newsy letters later) and limit your questions to those easily answered at this point. Thank your relative for his or her time, and strive for utmost courtesy in your writing. Some people feel that they are more likely to have a response if they include a self-addressed stamped envelope. When you receive a response, send a brief, sincere thank-you note.

Some people have found success including a form with their letter that lists several questions with room to "fill in the blank." If you ask simple, factual questions about names, dates, places, and events, your relatives don't have to try to decide what information to tell you; they just need to fill in the blanks. After you've "broken the ice" with your relatives, you may find greater success and more information as you continue to correspond.

Identify Your Family Historian

Many families have at least one individual who knows a significant amount of that family's history. This "gatekeeper" is perhaps the best source of a family's genealogical information. If you don't think your family has a gatekeeper, you can still gather information from family members even if they feel they know little about the family's history.

Sometimes a good family friend or an old neighbor can be a great source of information. You'll never know if you don't ask.

As you review the names on your list, ask yourself if there is one individual who strikes you as being a gatekeeper. Or perhaps there is an individual who has outlived all the other members of his or her immediate family. Does this person enjoy telling stories and have a knack for details? If possible, you may wish to begin with this person, whether your contact is by letter, e-mail, phone call, or in person. Your family gatekeeper might even have a computer file with your family tree.

Genealogy Jargon

Gatekeeper Usually an older member in an extended family who keeps much of the family knowledge and/or heirlooms.

Take Stock of Your Search

Congratulations! You have just completed Step One. Your family tree is starting to take shape. Depending on how much research others in your family have done, you may be well on your way to knowing about the lives of your ancestors and learning about your heritage.

Now you're ready for Step Two. You will be able to organize your findings using your *Family Tree Maker* software. Later, we will discuss how you can continue your research using both online and offline methods.

Step Two

Organize Your Information

In Step Two you will:

- Learn how to use your new *Family Tree Maker* (*FTM*) software to organize the information you have collected to this point.

- Explore the *Family Tree Maker* Web Search feature to discover information about your family.

Sandy Tackles the Paperwork

Sandy stood at her kitchen table, which could barely be seen beneath the piles of paper. "Not bad," she said with satisfaction. Only a few weeks before, she had known almost nothing about her family. Now she had quite a bit of information. If only she could organize it in some way that made sense to her.

Sandy had taken to heart the genealogist's golden rule: "Start with yourself." She had started with Worksheet A, writing down all her own information before moving onto B, C, and D, which asked for her parents' and grandparents' information. She also had a stack of papers about her husband's family.

She divided the papers into three piles: her father's family, her mother's family, and her husband's family. She knew little of her father's family, so it wouldn't take long to input his information using her new Family Tree Maker *software program. Her mother's information would take a little longer to enter. She could hardly wait to get started!*

Sandy has a good start on her research, so let's get started as well. You have two choices at this point. You may wish to go right to *Family Tree Maker (FTM)* and begin entering your information, or you may choose to copy your information first on a pedigree, or ancestral, chart. (see appendix, Form A).

Pedigree Chart

The pedigree, or ancestral, chart is one of the most well-known forms used by genealogists. The facing page shows a full five-generation chart, which allows you to see relationships between multiple generations of a family and trace your ancestry back in time along a particular family line.

A pedigree shows only your direct ancestors, not siblings, multiple marriages, or social family connections. This information appears on a different form, the family group sheet (see appendix, Form B). You may wish to transfer your family information to this sheet and from there enter the information into your new *FTM* software. However, once you enter your information in *FTM*, it will generate many forms for you, including the pedigree chart and the family group sheet.

Genealogy Jargon

Pedigree chart A register recording a line of ancestors.

Note: Genealogy forms like this pedigree chart can be downloaded free of charge from the Ancestry.com website at <www.ancestry.com/trees/charts/ancchart.aspx>. There are also worksheets and forms at the back of this book you can photocopy for personal use.

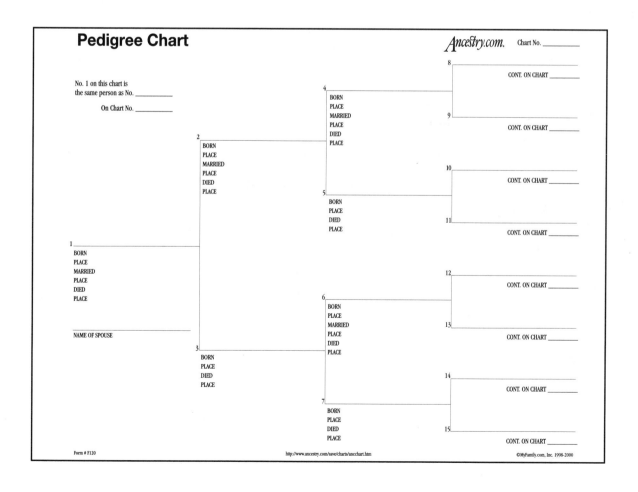

Enter Your Information into Family Tree Maker

To begin, place the CD into your computer's CD-ROM drive and follow the on-screen, step-by-step installation instructions. In order to take full advantage of all that *FTM* has to offer, be sure to register your *Family Tree Maker* software and activate your free Ancestry.com trial

Installation Launcher

membership. You can do this during installation or in the program—simply click **Register Family Tree Maker** from the **Help** menu.

You will be asked to enter your name and e-mail address and to create a password. For future reference, you may want to write your e-mail address and password below.

E-mail   _____

Password   _____

Your family "gatekeeper" may already have a computer file on your family. Most likely he or she can share this information with you in the form of a GEDCOM file, which can be opened in *FTM*. Click

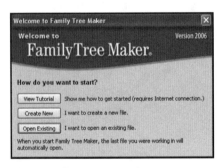

Welcome Screen

the **Open Existing** button on the Welcome Screen; or, in the program, click **Open** from the **File** menu. (The GEDCOM file must be saved to your hard drive before you can open it.) Select the location where you've placed the GEDCOM file. From the **Files of type** drop-down list, choose "GEDCOM(*.GED)". When you find the file, select it and click the **Open** button.

If you don't have a "gatekeeper" in your family, you'll need to start your file from scratch. Click the **New** button on the Welcome Screen; or, in the program, click **New** from the **File** menu. A dialog box will pop up that asks you to enter a name and select a location for your file.

Family Tree Maker uses two primary views for entering and viewing information: the Family View and Pedigree View. When your Family File opens, the first window to appear is the Family View.

About GEDCOM

Because computers give everyone the ability to organize thousands of records, the sharing of genealogical information has changed greatly as the number of records has increased. The problem comes when people attempt to share their information. The program your great-aunt uses to accumulate data may not be the same program you use, which could prevent you from sharing valuable information. Since many different genealogical software programs are available and not all genealogists use the same one, GEDCOM provides a way for genealogists to share information created in different programs.

GEDCOM stands for GEnealogical Data COMmunications. GEDCOM is a file format that allows genealogy files to be opened in any genealogy software program. Genealogists using a Macintosh program can save their information in a GEDCOM, which can be accessed by any genealogist using Windows-based software. The data you accumulate using *Family Tree Maker* software can be stored as a program file or as a set of files on your own computer. You can also export a Family File as a GEDCOM file and store it on your hard drive, a floppy disk, CD-ROM, or all of the above.

If you export the information to a removable floppy disk, that disk can then be given to anyone wishing to import the material into his or her own genealogy program. Your great-aunt or second cousin can then share what you've accumulated. And if they, or anyone else interested in your research, has e-mail access, you can send copies of what you've done as e-mail message attachments. You can also convert your GEDCOM file to HTML so you can put it on your Web page for others to share.

GEDCOM was developed and introduced in 1987 by The Church of Jesus Christ of Latter-day Saints.

Family View

The Family View lets you enter information about a family unit (husband, wife, and children) in a format that makes it easy to see the relationship between members of a family. At the top of the window are spaces for the names and vital information for both husband and wife. At the bottom of the window is space for the names of all the children of the husband and wife.

Family View

Starting with yourself, fill in the husband or wife fields with your name and date and place of birth. (You don't need to save your changes—*FTM* automatically saves your file as you work and when you close the file.) If you need help, you can click the **Help** button on the toolbar at any time.

Now click the **Edit** button for your entry. This will bring up an Edit Individual window. The information you have already entered about yourself appears on the General tab.

Edit Individual window

- If you would like to enter additional information about events in your life, click the **Facts** tab at the top of the window.

- To record notes about certain events, click the **Notes** tab at the top of the window.

- To record the source for a particular event, click the **S** or **Sources/Citations** button to the right of a field. Be sure to include the source of any information you add to your family tree. It is very likely that at some point you, or someone you share your files with, will need to retrace your steps. When you add a source, you can classify and define your sources (with fields that include author, title, publication facts, and library call number).

After you finish recording information about yourself, you are ready to input information about your marriage, children, parents, and siblings.

- To add a spouse, enter their information in the appropriate Husband or Wife fields.

- To record a marriage, enter a date and place in the Marriage fields.

- To add children, enter their names, birth dates and places, and additional information in the Children fields.

- To record information for parents, click the appropriate **+Add Parents** button and complete their fields.

Now that you've learned how to enter your information in the Family View, you can explore the other view in *Family Tree Maker*—the Pedigree View.

Pedigree View

The Pedigree View provides a more comprehensive view of your Family File. It lets you see several generations at once and provides an easy way to navigate to each member of your family tree. To go to the Pedigree View, click the **Pedigree View** button on the toolbar or choose **Pedigree View** from the **View** menu.

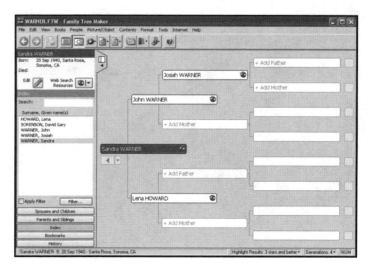

Pedigree View

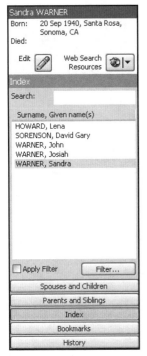

Pedigree View Side Panel

The person you last selected in the Family View will appear in the primary or "root" position of the pedigree tree, and their ancestors will branch to the right. If you don't appear as the root individual, click your name in the index of names on the left side of the pedigree tree. You should now appear as the root individual. You can use the various arrows to navigate to each individual's ancestors and descendants.

On the left side of the window, you'll notice the Pedigree View Side Panel. The Side Panel provides more information about whichever individual in the tree is selected; the details at the top of the Side Panel stay the same, while the main section of the Side Panel changes according to which button you click. You can view lists of an individual's spouse, children, parents, and siblings; all the individuals in your file; important individuals you've bookmarked; and a history of recently edited individuals.

Sandy Explores *Family Tree Maker*

As Sandy started typing her family names into the new software, she was curious about the small world icon that appeared by each name in the Pedigree View. What did it mean?

She clicked on the icon and in a few moments, a new window appeared that showed her several "hits," or possible matches, with her ancestor's name. She quickly scanned the list of names and found several that looked promising. Clicking on the search result, she saw some familiar names and dates from her research. She had a match!

The Web Search Feature

The Web Search feature lets you search the vast collection of databases on Ancestry.com to look for more information about individuals in your Family File—without ever leaving your *Family Tree Maker* software. Records regarding your ancestor may appear in census records, birth and death indexes, passenger lists, military records, or even in one of the many family and local histories on the site.

Note: To use the Web Search feature, you need a subscription to Ancestry.com (your free trial membership included with Family Tree Maker *will work) and an Internet connection.*

To view potential matches, click the **Web Search** button beside the name of your ancestor, or click **Web Search Results** from the **View** menu.

Web Search icon in the Pedigree View

After searching for a moment, the Web Search Results will appear. The top half of the screen will show a list of the different records located on Ancestry.com that might match your ancestor. Remember that the greater the number of stars next to the record, the better the match will be. The bottom half of the screen lets you compare, side-by-side, details about the highlighted record with the information you have in your Family File.

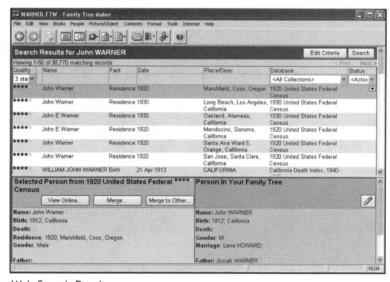

Web Search Results

As you review the suggested matches, compare the information with what you already know about the individual and his or her family; for example, where or when do you believe this person was born, where did he or she live and die, and so on. While this feature can be challenging, it can provide many avenues of research in a short amount of time.

Merge Web Search Results into Your Family File

If you examine the potential matches offered in the Web Search Results and find a record that matches your family member, you don't

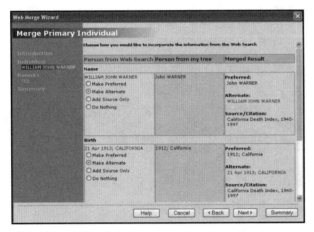

Web Merge Wizard

have to write down the information and enter it into the software yourself; you can merge that information into your Family File using your *FTM* software. Simply click the **Merge** button and follow the instructions in the Web Merge Wizard. And best of all, source information will be included automatically.

Make Backups of Your Work

It is always a good idea to keep copies or backups of your work, both on paper and on disk. To make a backup of your new *FTM* file, click **Backup** from the **File** menu. Choose a backup method—hard drive, floppy disk, CD-ROM, or Internet—and click the **Backup** button. *FTM* will make a copy of the current file you are working in.

That's it! You have just used some basic features of the *Family Tree Maker* software that you will need to organize your family history. You may feel like a stranger in unknown territory for a while, but the more you move about in the software, the more comfortable you'll feel and the more you'll learn about its other helpful features.

Family Tree Maker includes on online tutorial that illustrates and explains how to use its many powerful features. To access the tutorial, choose **Getting Started Tutorial** from the **Help** menu. In addition, a thorough user guide, *The Official Guide to Family Tree Maker*, is available for purchase at <www.theancestrystore.com>.

Focus on One Ancestor or Family

By now you have gathered enough information to realize that you can't research everyone at once. This is the time to make a choice. Ask yourself, "Which family line do I want to pursue?" Once you decide, choose a key individual who will be your main point of interest. Choosing this person may mean closing your eyes and pointing at the pedigree chart, or you may feel driven to search out a certain family line. However and whomever you choose, be sure to record all of the results from online searches about your key individual, print the screen with the information source, and keep it with your research log.

Congratulations! You have made a terrific start in building your family tree. Before you continue on to Step Three, you may want to spend more time investigating Ancestry.com to familiarize yourself with the website and its resources. You may also want to browse through the suggested trees and records for your other ancestors before you choose which ancestor to focus on. When you are ready to continue, you'll find even more exciting discoveries ahead!

Step Three

Search for Your Ancestors

In Step Three you will:

- Learn how to use various records to obtain information about your ancestors.

- Become familiar with online family trees to help you make connections with possible family members and expand your research.

- Use message boards and mailing lists to learn more about your family history.

Sandy Strikes Gold

Sitting at her computer, Sandy looked at her worksheets and noted the blank spaces. She knew almost nothing about her grandfather's family. Her grandfather had died years before, and she couldn't remember him ever talking about his parents.

Sandy was feeling hopeful when she signed on to the Internet and typed "www.ancestry.com" in the address bar. The Ancestry.com homepage came up and she clicked the "Historical Records" tab. Then she typed her grandfather's name in the search boxes, and waited, hoping she would be able to find her grandfather's name in one of the databases.

When a list of potential matches appeared on the page, she saw that the Social Security Death Index had found seven people with the same name as her grandfather. With her trial subscription, Sandy had access to this database so she clicked on the link. Seven names appeared on the screen; each name gave date of birth, date of death, and last residence.

Since beginning her family quest, Sandy had learned that her grandfather had been born in Michigan, not California as she had always believed. Sandy studied the list and was rewarded when she found her grandfather's name and correct birthplace at the bottom of the list. She clicked the link to view the record.

His Social Security number had been issued in Michigan. That was not really a surprise. What startled Sandy was her grandfather's birth date, which was eight years earlier than he had indicated on the 1930 census. Had he lied on the census? Or had the census taker talked to someone in the household who hadn't known the real date? What was Grandpa doing all that time in Michigan? And when did he move to California?

Sandy clicked on the link to "Request copy of original application," wondering what she could learn from this source. The next page gave instructions on how to request information from the Social Security Administration. It also listed the information that might be found on her grandfather's Social Security application.

Sandy was excited as she clicked on the link to generate a written request for information. Her grandfather's application should have his date of birth and his parents' names. She might have just found the key to unlock the next generation on his line.

Explore Records on Ancestry.com

As your family tree continues to grow, you will want to move on to new sources and methods of research, which will be discussed here. You may feel apprehensive as you leave your comfort zone, but if you persevere you will soon discover some of the wonderful rewards of genealogy.

As you learned in Step Two, you can access databases at Ancestry.com using the Web Search feature in *Family Tree Maker*; you can also go straight to the website to search for your family. Ancestry.com offers a large variety of records including birth and death indexes, city and county directories, regiment musters, and even personal histories. Many are specific to time and

Record Types at Ancestry.com

Ancestry.com has thousands of unique databases covering many different time periods and locations with more being added weekly. While these databases are just a portion of all the records you can find when looking for your ancestors, they include a wide variety of records. These databases include the following types of records:

Almanacs
Alumni lists
Autobiographies
Biographies
Burial records
Cemetery records
Census records
County histories
Diaries
Directories
Emigration records
Family histories
Family trees
Gazetteers
Genealogical registers
Immigrant records and port arrivals
Indexes to birth and death records
Journals
Land claims and records
Maps
Naturalization records
Newspapers
Obituary lists
Parish records
Personal histories
Service roster
Ships passenger lists
Tax records and indexes
Town histories
University directories
Veteran lists
Voter lists
War records
Wills

place and are helpful if you can locate your ancestor within that time and place.

The amount of information available on the Ancestry.com website is constantly growing. If you don't find what you're looking for today, try again next week, and again next month. If you encounter a "brick wall" with one ancestor's line, look for your ancestor's siblings. Families often lived near one another and moved together from one place to another. If you are able to locate a sibling, you may find the ancestor you are seeking.

Two valuable resources collected by the U.S. federal government are the Social Security Death Index (SSDI) and the U.S. censuses. Records gathered by city, county, and state government agencies include birth, marriage, and death records (called vital records) as well as land records. These types are records are all available on Ancestry.com.

Social Security Death Index (SSDI)

The Social Security Administration has indexed the deaths of more than 79 million people into one of the largest databases available: the Social Security Death Index, or SSDI. The index is a database created by the federal government that has proven valuable to genealogists. Since 1935, when Franklin D. Roosevelt signed the Social Security Act into law, the government has issued more than 440 million Social Security numbers. As the numbers indicate, not everyone who was issued a Social Security number is in the SSDI.

Genealogy Jargon

Social Security Death Index (SSDI) A database that contains the records of deceased persons who possessed Social Security numbers and whose deaths have been reported to the Social Security Administration since 1962.

Nevertheless, the SSDI is a great source to track down information about family members who have passed away within the last fifty years.

One reason the SSDI is so valuable is because it is often a stepping-stone to other records, such as obituaries, cemetery records, and official death records. The original application should list information about your ancestor, including the names of both parents. If you are able to locate the date and place of death from the SSDI, then more records are opened up to further your investigation.

The SSDI is available online at Ancestry.com at <www.ancestry.com/search/db.aspx?dbid=3693>. Or simply go to the homepage at Ancestry.com, and click on the "Search" tab at the top of the screen. Then click "Social Security Death Index" under the "Birth, Marriage & Death" heading on the right side of the page. (You can also access the SSDI for free at RootsWeb <http://ssdi.rootsweb.com>.)

Tips of the Trade

If you find a record on Ancestry.com that you want to add to your *FTM* Family File, you don't have to enter the information manually. You can use the Web Search feature to find the record on Ancestry.com. Then, you can merge the information into your Family File, including source citations and images.

When you search for a particular ancestor, the matches in the database will appear on the page. After you have located your ancestor, click the "Request copy of original application" link. This link will take you to a page where you can write a letter to the Social Security

Charles Lindbergh's Social Security number application

Administration. Ancestry.com automatically generates a letter you can print out, which requests a copy of your ancestor's original application for a Social Security number. This letter will contain all the pertinent data necessary to obtain information on the individual you are researching. All you need to do is sign your name, include the fee made payable to the Social Security Administration, and drop the letter in the mail.

Tips of the Trade

The Social Security Administration charges a fee for a copy of your ancestor's original application.

Census Records

A census is an official count of a population. In the United States, the federal government and many state governments have conducted censuses in one form or another since the eighteenth century. The first U.S. federal population census was conducted in 1790, and a population census has been conducted every ten years since that time. However, due to privacy concerns, federal law prohibits the release of records for seventy-two years after their creation.

The 1930 census, released in April 2002, is the most recent federal census available to researchers. The 1930 census images are exclusively available at Ancestry.com, with some 123 million names. Along with the 1930 census, Ancestry.com offers all of the U.S. federal censuses from 1790 to 1920, some 13 million images.

Census Secrets

Do you wonder when your ancestors came to America? Check the 1900, 1910, 1920, and 1930 censuses. They list a person's year of immigration and the citizenship status of the person, with codes AL for alien, PA for first papers filed, and NA for naturalized.

Most people today probably knew someone who was alive in 1930—parents, grandparents, aunts, uncles, teachers, or possibly even employers and coworkers, which makes the 1930 census even more exciting.

A 1900 census schedule

Although census records were never intended to become genealogical records, they are a real boon to genealogists, who can use the census records to track their ancestors. State censuses may also be helpful, although they differ from year to year and state to state, depending on various factors.

The questions that census takers asked have changed over the years and before the 1850 census, only heads of households were listed by name. Other questions can give you information about immigration, occupation, race, literacy, language, and whether the family home

Soundex Help

The Soundex is an index that was first developed to help with census researching. It uses fixed rules to code surnames to compensate for variant spellings. At Ancestry.com, some databases are searchable by Soundex. Simply checking this option will find results for names that sound like the name you enter in the search box. This approach is particularly effective with names that have variants based on English-language phonics.

was owned or rented. See <www.ancestry.com/learn/library/article.aspx?article=1264> for a list of the questions asked for each census year.

The wonderful thing about census research is that the federal census records are readily available for each decade from 1790 through 1930, except for the 1890 census records, which were destroyed in a fire. Ancestry.com offers every-name indexes and images for all the available censuses—from 1790 to 1930. (This is a paid subscription service.)

Census films can also be viewed at the National Archives in Washington, D.C., major libraries, and the Family History Library in Salt Lake City, Utah. The films can be borrowed from the Family History Library through your local Family History Center. (See <www.familysearch.org> for a location near you.) Some state websites offer the census information for their state as well.

Since one of the rules of sound genealogical research is to start with yourself and work backward in time, moving from the known to the unknown, you'll want to start with the most recent census available. Were your parents alive in 1930? Where were they living? Start with them, and when you have exhausted this resource, move to the 1920 census and look for family members who were alive at that time.

A useful resource to help you with census records is *Finding Answers in U.S. Census Records* by Loretto Dennis Szucs and Matthew Wright (Ancestry, 2002).

Census Secrets

The 1900 and 1920 censuses show if a person is a Civil War veteran or the widow of a veteran. Learning this information can lead you to the veteran's military and pension files. The 1930 census also asks questions about military service.

Tips of the Trade

Census forms to record the information you find, as well as other genealogical forms, can be downloaded free of charge at <www.ancestry.com/charts/census.aspx>.

Vital Records

Vital records are records of life events important enough that some level of government acquires, organizes, and preserves them. They can be found at either the local, county, or state level. In genealogy, the term "vital record" refers specifically to birth, marriage, and death events. As a general rule, these records are maintained locally. In most of the United States, the city, town, or county maintains the records. Since the end of the nineteenth century, many states also began keeping records of each of these events. These are maintained at the state's capital city by an office of vital records, vital statistics, etc.

The *Red Book: American State, County, and Town Sources* by Alice Eichholz (Ancestry, 2004) is a great resource for learning how to locate these record-keeping entities by county. Another useful book is *The Ancestry Family Historian's Address Book* by Juliana S. Smith (Ancestry, 2003).

A useful place to learn about what records are available and where you can order copies is <www.vitalrec.com>. This site is organized by state and lists addresses of the agencies that hold the records. There are charts on the site that detail the record type available, the dates covered by the records, any fees associated with acquiring copies, additional remarks, and a convenient order form.

In some cases, these vital records have been indexed to help genealogists locate specific records more easily. Some indexes are available online at various genealogical websites. In many areas, vital records have been preserved on microfilm and may be found in public libraries or ordered from the Family History Library, which circulates more than

> **Genealogy Jargon**
>
> **Vital Records** Civil records of life events (birth, marriage, death) preserved by an official source (e.g., county governments).

> **Did You Know?**
>
> Birth, marriage, and death records are the foundation of genealogical research. What we learn from the vital records of a person's life provides the framework for our search for other records that may illuminate his or her life and times.

Birth Records

In the United States, birth records are modern records. They seldom exist prior to 1900, except in the New England states.

100,000 rolls of film each month through its numerous Family History Centers. The library itself has more than 2.4 million rolls of microfilmed genealogical records and 742,000 microfiche, a collection that is steadily growing.

A 1901 birth record

Birth Records. Most birth records, especially earlier ones, contain only basic information. In an early New England birth record, for example, you are likely to find the name of the child, date and place of birth, and parents' names. By the mid-nineteenth century, birth records generally became more informative.

Marriage Records. Ironically, in some states the government required that marriage records be kept before birth and death records were required. This stems from the legal implications of property ownership in a marriage. There are many types of marriage records since a marriage is usually a multi-step process. This gives you many different opportunities to find records to learn about your ancestors.

Marriage Licenses

Traditionally, applying for and securing a license to marry provided an opportunity to determine whether or not the couple met certain conditions. One condition was that the agreement to marry was made without coercion. Another was age requirements. A third was consanguinity. In most states, marriages cannot be made between relations closer than first cousins. Knowing the law governing marriage in the state and during the time period of your search is a great help in finding and interpreting the records. Keep in mind that the application for or the granting of a license, with or without a consent form, is not proof that the marriage occurred. It means only that the couple sought or received a license to marry.

Marriage Records
The marriage license is the most common marriage record in the United States.

Record of a Civil Marriage

Once any requirements for consent and bonds were met, the couple was granted a license to marry. They then sought someone authorized to perform the marriage ceremony. This could be a church official or someone in the county, such as a Justice of the Peace, who was legally able to conduct the marriage. The officiating body then filed a "return of marriage," usually with the county that had issued the license.

The Marriage Ceremony

If a marriage was conducted by a representative of a particular church or denomination, the church register would have noted the ceremony. Some denominations may have had a special book to record services such as christenings, marriages, and burials. Or the marriage may have been noted in a general book that was a

Marriage Bond.

THE COMMONWEALTH OF KENTUCKY.

Be it Known, that we, *Cornelius Guilfoil* as principal, and *Michael Sweeney* as surety, are jointly and severally bound to the Commonwealth of Kentucky, in the sum of One Hundred Dollars.

The Condition of this Bond is as follows:

That, whereas Marriage is intended to be solemnized between the above bound *Cornelius Guilfoil* and *Rosanna Sweeney* Now, if there is no lawful cause to obstruct said marriage, this bond shall be void, otherwise it shall remain in full force and effect. Dated at Maysville, Mason County, this *25th*.

Kentucky marriage bond

Tips of the Trade

Can't find the marriage record for your great-grandparents? Look for it in the bride's home county or town of residence. Always check for the formal marriage license application, not just for marriage certificates and the filed returns.

day-to-day recording of church activities. A church recording usually supplements a civil recording and may provide different information about the bride and groom or their parents' involvement with the church.

Proof of Marriage

Three records verify that a marriage took place: a marriage return recorded in a civil register, an entry of marriage in a church register, and a certificate given to the couple by the individual who performed the ceremony. The latter, often decorative and suitable for display, is often found in the family's possession.

A marriage return is made by the official who conducted the marriage. The notation of a return may be found in the license application book in a space provided. The pages in such a book, generally referred to as a register of marriages, may be pre-printed in quarters.

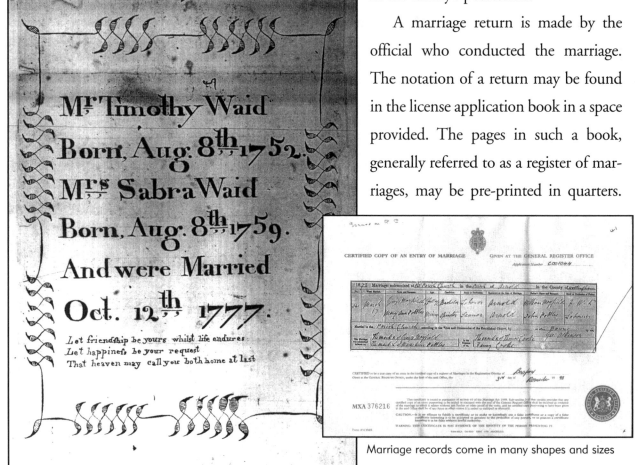

Marriage records come in many shapes and sizes

The top two quarters are the license application and any affidavits. The lower half is a form for a bond and space to enter the information from the marriage return. The lack of a return does not necessarily mean that the couple didn't marry. There are many reasons for failure to file a return, including the difficulty of travel for those who officiated in rural or frontier areas.

> **Tips of the Trade**
>
> Learning the religious affiliation of your ancestors can open up a whole new world of church and religious records. Religious leaders often kept records of important happenings in their communities, especially surrounding the births, marriages, and deaths of members.

The ideal marriage record gives the full names of the bride and groom; the full names of the parents (including mothers' maiden names) of both bride and groom; the ages of the parties to be wed; the towns in which they were residents; the occupations of employed parties; the place and date of the ceremony; the person who officiated at the marriage; and the full names and residences of any witnesses. Although this detail is seldom found for any single marriage record, combining civil and church records will often provide most of the information.

Locate Marriage Records

During the early part of the twentieth century, many states began to require that a record of the marriage be transferred from the county to the state level. For the years since this procedure came fully into effect, it may be possible to search a statewide index.

To find civil marriage records for any time period, consult *Red Book* (Ancestry, 2004) or visit <www.vitalrec.com>. The *Red Book* will help you identify the county of jurisdiction at the time of the wedding.

> **Marriage Records**
>
> Marriage certificates are generally given to the couple after the ceremony and are usually found among family records. The marriage license application is usually on file in the town or county clerk's office where the couple was married or where they obtained the license.

Death Records. In certain times and places you may find that death records give only the name of the deceased, the date of death, and the place of death. The best records will list details such as age, occupation, marital status, place of birth, cause of death, place of burial, and more.

Death Records

If you can't find a death certificate, look for information about the individual's death in the family Bible or newspaper obituaries. Don't forget to check funeral homes and cemeteries for burial records and tombstone inscriptions.

Obituary records and cemetery records may give you additional information—usually about survivors—but they may not be as easily found as death records.

To supplement your quest for civil death records, look for these additional sources:

- Bible records and other family papers
- Court records (wills and administrations)
- Census records (mortality schedules)
- Military service and pension records
- Newspapers (death notices, obituaries, and news articles)
- Cemetery records and tombstone inscriptions

Register of Deaths at the New York

Gen'l. Register Number	Name	Rank	Co.	Regiment or Vessel	Nativity
1449.	Christian Weigel	Private	"I"	25th Reg. N.Y.V.	Germany
104	James Maloney.	Private	"I"	140th Reg. N.Y.V.	Ireland
	James Crelly.	Private	"H"	111th Reg. N.Y.V.	U.S.
14.	Edward Hayes.	Private	"C"	100th Reg. N.Y.V.	Ireland.
hqu.	Edward Grass.	Private	"C"	1st Cav. N.Y.V. 2nd Reg. N.Y.V.	Germany
h14.	John Agan.	Private	"A"	8th Cav. N.Y.V. 24th Reg.	Ireland.
nng.	George Miller.	Private	"K"	14th H. Arty. N.Y.V.	Germany.

A register of New York deaths

Online Family Trees

Online family trees are pedigree files (usually GEDCOMs) that researchers just like you have submitted to a website. Because users all over the world can upload their family trees, it is easier than ever to find and share your family history. By creating your own online tree or searching for trees, you may be brought into contact with others who are researching the same ancestral lines. If you find a common ancestor, you can add branches to your family tree instantly. Two collections of user-submitted family trees can be accessed at Ancestry.com—Member Trees and Community Trees.

> ### Personal and Public Member Trees
> Ancestry.com members can choose to make their Member Trees personal or public. Both types of trees are searchable, but only Public Member Trees can be viewed by others. If a match is located on a Personal Member Tree, you will be provided with only the owner's contact information.

Member Trees

Member Trees are personal family trees created or submitted by individuals and stored online at Ancestry.com. People have been creating personal family trees since July of 2006. More than 1.5 million trees have been created so far and more than 50,000 new trees are added each month. Members can choose to make their trees personal or public.

> ### Genealogy Jargon
> **Database** A collection of information organized for rapid search and retrieval with a computer.

Community Trees

Community Trees—previously known as Ancestry Family Tree (a database of user-submitted family trees) and OneWorldTree (a family tree and historical records search engine) can still be searched for matches to your family tree; however, you can no longer add family trees to these databases.

Search Member and Community Trees

To access the millions of names found in Member and Community Trees, go to the Ancestry.com homepage and click the "Family Trees" search tab. In the blank name fields, enter the name of the key individual whom you are researching. Click the Search button and you will see results for both Member Trees and Community Trees.

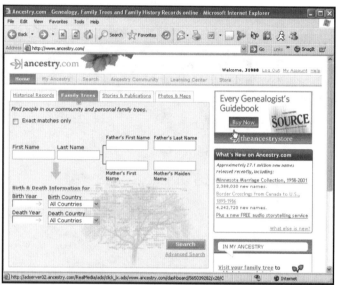

Member and Community Tree search

If this name brings up a large number of matches, you may want to limit your search. Try adding another variable, such as a spouse's name. (If you include several variables and one of them is wrong, the search may eliminate the ancestor you are looking for.)

If the searching brings up very few or no matches, try variant spellings of the name. For example, the name Isaacson could also be spelled as Isackson, Isacksen, Isaakson, Isakson, and so on. Try searching the last name only, or if the first name is very unusual, try a search by first name (it is helpful to limit this kind of search by place or date).

If you don't have much success at first, don't be discouraged—and remember to keep track of each search on a Research Log (Worksheet E).

Analyze the Matches

Take the time to analyze the different trees that you find; as you consider each possible match, look at the information available and compare the match with other information you already know—such as spouse's name and dates for birth, marriage, and death, as well as locations for these events.

If you find a solid match, some services let you download a GEDCOM of the tree, thus eliminating the need to recopy it. Remember that the information you download from any online family tree will need to be checked for accuracy and reliability. Not all researchers are as careful as they should be. Since online data can come from a variety of sources, it needs to be thoroughly verified before you accept it as accurate.

> ### Tips of the Trade
>
> Family trees on Ancestry.com will never share information about living family members born after 1930. Any information in your family tree regarding living people born after 1930 will show up on your personal family tree but will remain hidden from other Ancestry.com members.

Most genealogists import information from other sources into a new file, rather than directly into their own file. This allows them to have ready access to others' information without accepting potentially inaccurate information as part of their own research. If you choose to merge one of these online trees with your database, select a family tree with good source citations so that you can verify their findings more easily.

Additional Features

You have just learned some of the basic ways you can use online family trees to enhance your family history. But there's more. For example, you can use the Ancestry.com "Connection Service" to anonymously contact others who have contributed family trees, and, you can attach records you find to individuals in your online tree. To learn more about the many features available in online trees, click the "Learning Center" tab at the top of any Ancestry.com page. Then, in the "Learn More About" section on the right-hand side of the page, click the "Family Trees" link.

Sandy Makes a Connection

After learning more about her grandfather from his Social Security number application, Sandy decided to focus her efforts on her grandfather's father,

Josiah Warner. She began by searching for his surname in the message boards at Ancestry.com. Although she saw numerous hits, her eye was caught by a message board listing about Warners who lived in the same county where her grandfather had lived in 1920. "Could they be related?" she wondered. She decided to e-mail John Warner, the man who had posted the message online.

After a brief e-mail exchange, Sandy was able to determine that this man was her father's first cousin—the son of her father's uncle by a second marriage that no one in the family had known about.

Sandy was stunned but delighted. She hadn't thought that there were any living relatives on her father's side, and here she had found her father's cousin and his family. John was an avid genealogist, and he offered to share his research with her in a GEDCOM file. Sandy and John started monthly telephone conversations to give each other research updates. John even invited Sandy to the next family reunion. She could hardly wait to meet him in person and spend some time with her father's extended family.

Use the Internet to Share Your Search

Despite hours of research, sometimes one elusive ancestor stubbornly refuses to come out of hiding. What can you do? One suggestion is to turn your attention to another ancestor. Time often allows other records to surface, and by the time you return to this particular ancestor, these records may have been microfilmed or perhaps even uploaded to a website.

Another option is to review and analyze all the information you have up to this point. You may see some connections surfacing or some new areas of research opening up.

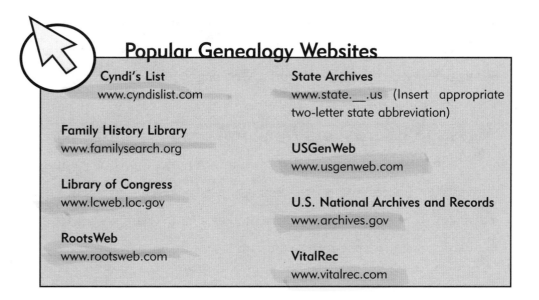

Popular Genealogy Websites

Cyndi's List
www.cyndislist.com

Family History Library
www.familysearch.org

Library of Congress
www.lcweb.loc.gov

RootsWeb
www.rootsweb.com

State Archives
www.state.___.us (Insert appropriate two-letter state abbreviation)

USGenWeb
www.usgenweb.com

U.S. National Archives and Records
www.archives.gov

VitalRec
www.vitalrec.com

RootsWeb

RootsWeb, sponsored by The Generations Network, Inc., is the result of millions of online genealogists sharing research. Users can submit transcribed data from their own research and add their own family tree to a database containing hundreds of millions of names. New databases are added to RootsWeb regularly, so you will want to check back frequently.

You may want to begin by looking through the links in the Getting Started section (see "Getting Started at RootsWeb" and "RootsWeb's Guide to Tracing Family Trees"). You'll find directions for communicating with others and submitting your own research, as well as guides to vital records and locality research.

You can also subscribe to the *RootsWeb Review*, browse through past issues of the

RootsWeb homepage

Review in the archives, and learn about the website's new databases in the "What's New" section. RootsWeb also links to tens of thousands of genealogical websites and individual Web pages.

Message Boards and Mailing Lists

Mailing lists and message boards allow genealogists with common interests to "meet" and share their knowledge, even their genealogy databases. You may find a group devoted to a family name or a particular locale where an ancestor was known to reside.

Message Boards

A message board is a lot like an old-fashioned bulletin board that you access through the Internet. Ancestry.com is home to more than 175,000 message boards on a wide range of topics—surnames, localities, adoptions, shipwrecks, occupations, and more. Posting a message on the appropriate message board allows other researchers to learn of your search and invites them to share their ideas and experience. For guidelines to writing good queries, see "Netiquette for Family Historians" on the facing page. If you have questions about the message boards at Ancestry.com, click the "Help" link in the top, right-hand corner of the Ancestry.com homepage. Then enter the topic "message boards" to access a list of frequently asked questions.

> **Genealogy Jargon**
>
> **Message Board** An Internet tool that allows people to "talk" with others who have similar interests. Message boards offer a website where people can post their comments and questions.

Mailing Lists

A mailing list is like an e-mail party line, where every message that a list subscriber sends to the list is distributed to all other list

Netiquette for Family Historians

Mailing lists and message boards are a tremendous boon to genealogists. Your query will be read by thousands of people, so you will have a good chance of learning something about your family history that you didn't already know. The possibilities are definitely exciting. But before you start writing, take some time to explore the website that hosts the mailing list or message board, click on the links that look interesting, read the guidelines, browse the index of names and topics for both mailing lists and message boards, and review former posts submitted by subscribers.

Some Guidelines

Join only one or two lists to begin with. Some lists generate as many as fifty to one hundred posts per day. It can take a lot of time to go through that many e-mails. It also means that when you post your message, it may not be posted immediately. So be patient.

You can subscribe to either Mail or Digest mode. Mail will cause your mailbox to fill up more quickly so choose it only if you plan to check your e-mail daily and delete your e-mail frequently. Choose Digest if you want fewer e-mails, since individual e-mails will be combined in one large e-mail.

You need to subscribe and belong to a list in order to post. It is wise to wait a while before submitting a message.

A week or so will let you get a feel for the kinds of messages posted here.

Remember to be polite and courteous, even when you disagree with another message. The list is very strict about its "no flaming" rule: that is no rude, abusive, emotional, or insulting messages may be posted. Those guilty of flaming will be taken off the list.

Compose your queries carefully. Remember that you are asking for help from someone you don't know. Be clear, courteous, and to the point.

Give names, dates, places, and sources. Tell what you know, where you have looked, and what you are looking for. Put surnames in all caps in subject lines and the first time it is used in the body of your query (e.g., Kristine Marie THOMSEN, Skallerup, Denmark, to New Orleans, ca. 1852).

Use all caps for names only. If you use it for anything else, it's hard to read and it looks like shouting.

Don't write in all lower case either. It can also be hard to read.

Separate information into paragraphs. This is easier to read than one solid page with no breaks.

Giving too much information is as unhelpful as giving too little. Don't give your whole family history or send GEDCOM files with your queries.

subscribers. There are more than 30,000 genealogy-related mailing lists on RootsWeb covering surnames, U.S. counties and states, countries and regions, ethnic groups, and other topics. If you have questions about the mailing lists at RootsWeb, click the "Help" tab on the top, right-hand corner of the homepage and scroll down to "Mailing Lists."

Successful Library Research

While genealogists may find a lot of information online, there comes a time in every genealogist's research when there is no substitute for a trip to the library. Many libraries and archives have a website that can supply information about days and hours of operation. Some even have online catalogues, so you can prepare ahead of time to make the most of your time on site.

> ### Genealogy Jargon
>
> **Family History Library (FHL)** The main genealogy library for The Church of Jesus Christ of Latter-day Saints, the Family History Library contains the world's largest collection of genealogical holdings, containing print sources and microfilmed records as well as records and other information shared by genealogists and family historians throughout the world.

While many genealogists travel to Salt Lake City to visit the Family History Library, family historians have access to almost all the records available there through the more than 3,400 satellite Family History Centers around the world. These centers have microfilm readers, and their volunteer staff will order microfilm records from the main library. To locate the family history center closest to you, visit the library's website at <www.familysearch.org>.

Wherever your research takes you, there are certain fundamentals of library research genealogists need to be aware of. If the library or archives center does not have a website, you will avoid some potential stumbling blocks if you call before you make a special trip and gather some important information. For example, is there an orientation tour of the library? Do you need to sign up in advance? Orientation sessions can save hours of valuable time by helping you learn what is available and where to find it. You will also meet a staff member who might be a good contact person to answer questions that may arise later.

Does the library have any special requirements like picture ID or local residency? Is it necessary to sign up in advance to use special equipment, such as microfilm and microfiche readers, or computers? Is parking available and what does it cost?

Are laptops allowed in the library? Many researchers bring their laptops with them, but you should check first to find out what the library's policy is on portable computers. If they are allowed, remember to carry all of your valuables with you when you leave your workspace.

Have a Plan

In addition to taking the essential research tools with you to the library, the most important item you can bring on your library trip is a plan.

When you plan your library trip, begin by writing down a list of records and what you hope to find in each one. (If the website gives catalog numbers, you can save yourself some time by writing these down or printing them out and attaching them to your plan.)

You may want to check the vital records for one individual or investigate the locality of the particular family you are researching. Two important rules to remember are:

- Start with yourself and work backward.

- Later records are easier to find than early records.

Essential Library Tools

Pencils. It's always a good idea to use a pencil in your preliminary research. In fact, some libraries require researchers to use only pencil.

Reading glasses. Some of the material that one discovers can be difficult to read even under the best conditions.

Magnifying glass. Some material is difficult to read even with good light and a good pair of glasses. A magnifying glass or magnifying bar can help.

Blank research forms or a laptop computer. Once you discover useful material, you need to record this information. Putting the information directly on research forms or into the computer cuts down one step.

Change. Photocopy machines usually take change or require a photocopy card. Carry some extra cash and a roll of coins so you can copy things you find.

Pedigree chart. You'll want to verify names and dates.

Family group sheet. At times your "key individual" won't show up in your research; names of siblings may help you locate ancestors since families often migrated together.

Also, American records may be more familiar and thus easier to locate than those from other countries. Genealogy is often a matter of searching for, analyzing, and discarding possibilities. Each of these takes time. Be patient with yourself and your plan.

Conclusion

Congratulations! You have successfully completed the training in *1-2-3 Family Tree*. With the knowledge you have gained, you should be able to make great strides in your family history research. You'll be amazed at the satisfaction you will feel upon learning the names of your ancestors and seeing their records, perhaps even their signatures, that were written decades or even centuries ago. The more you learn about your ancestors, the more you will learn about yourself and the better you will understand the foundation to your life—one that has been under construction for centuries by the ancestors who came before you. They are just waiting to be discovered. Happy hunting!

The Next Step

Our ancestors left behind a lot of information about themselves without realizing it. You can gain a wealth of information from a wide range of documentation. The following record types are good places to start when you are ready to take the next step.

Court Records

Court records are used primarily to get more extensive information about a person for whom you already know the essential dates. If you think there may be a court proceeding in a person's life (e.g., the individual was divorced), court records may provide a helpful avenue of research. Listed below are a few of the main court records that may be helpful to pursue.

Adoptions	Divorce
Apprenticeships	Guardianships
Bankruptcies	Land disputes
Civil cases	Naturalization records
Civil War claims	Orphan records
Criminal cases	Probate

Probate Records. When a person dies, state law provides for public supervision over the estate, whether or not there is a will. The term "probate records" broadly covers all the records produced by these laws, although, strictly speaking, "probate" applies only when there is a will. Family historians use probate case files more than any other kind of court record because probate tends to include so much personal data and because Americans have depended on the courts to settle their estates since North America was colonized. Probate files can be found in courthouses and archives across the United States.

Immigration and Naturalization Records

Most Americans can trace their family history back to an ancestor who entered this country as an immigrant. Estimates place the total number of immigrants to this country (from 1607 to the present) between 35 and 50 million. Knowing the immigrant's full name, approximate birth date, and the country of origin are the key pieces of information needed for tracking

immigration records. Two general references to help you with your search are *They Became Americans: Finding Naturalization Records and Ethnic Origins*, by Loretto Dennis Szucs, and *They Came in Ships*, by John P. Colletta.

Land Records

Land records have long provided genealogists with a way to bypass a dead-end family line. Land records are plentiful, accessible, easy-to-use, and interesting.

First, you must determine where your ancestor may have owned land (the state, county, and even the town). If you are uncertain where your ancestor lived, use census records to find the information. Then determine what types of land records exist for that locality and where you might find them. Most land records in the United States are kept at the county level.

To locate land records, you will need the following information:

- an accurate date and place,
- name of the individual(s) purchasing the land, and
- where the individual(s) was living when the purchase occurred.

You can learn more about this vast and fascinating group of records by reading *Land and Property Research in the United States* by E. Wade Hone.

Military Records

Most American families can claim at least one family member who has served in the United States military. Various types of records were created for every individual who served in the military. The challenges are learning what and where these records are, and how to use them as a research aid. To obtain information about individuals who served in the military, contact the National Archives in Washington, D.C. An excellent resource for finding military records is *U.S Military Records* by James C. Neagles.

The books mentioned above can all be ordered online at <www.theancestrystore.com> or by calling 1-800-ANCESTRY (262-3787).

Appendixes

Glossary

Census An official listing of a population. Federal censuses are taken every ten years in the United States. The dates for state censuses vary.

Community Trees Family trees submitted to Ancestry.com before Member Trees were available. These trees are housed in Ancestry World Tree and OneWorldTree and are searchable online.

Database A collection of information organized for rapid search and retrieval with a computer.

Emigrant One who leaves a country or region to settle in another area.

Family History Centers Local genealogical centers available to family historians throughout the world. Patrons can order microfilm from the Family History Library for use in the center at its microfilm readers for the minimal cost of shipping. See Family History Library (FHL).

Family History Library (FHL) The main genealogy library for The Church of Jesus Christ of Latter-day Saints (LDS or the Mormons), the Family History Library contains the world's largest collection of genealogical holdings, containing both print sources and microfilmed records, as well as records and other information shared by genealogists and family historians throughout the world.

Gatekeeper Usually an older member in an extended family who keeps much of the family knowledge and/or heirlooms.

GEDCOM Acronym for GEnealogical Data COMmunication. The standard file format used by family tree software to facilitate information sharing.

Generation A single step in the line of descent from an ancestor.

Given name A first and middle name.

Global search A general search of all databases in a collection, like the one used at Ancestry.com.

Immigrant One who settles in a country having emigrated from another country.

Index A list of names or records compiled from primary sources.

Land record A record showing the buyer and seller of a piece of property.

Member Trees Family trees uploaded to or created on Ancestry.com by members. Trees can be made personal (only viewable by the creator) or public (viewable by anyone).

Message board An Internet tool that allows people to "talk" together with others who have similar interests. Message boards offer a website where people can post their comments and questions.

Naturalization record An official government record showing when and where an alien became a U.S. citizen.

Pedigree chart A register recording a line of ancestors.

Primary source A record of an event by an eyewitness to that event at or near the time the event occurred.

Probate records Court records that deal with the settling of one's estate after death.

Query A question asked about an ancestor to an unknown audience in order to receive confirmation or new information.

Research log A written record detailing your research progress.

Secondary source A written record of an event created sometime after the event occurred.

Social Security Death Index (SSDI) A database that contains the records of deceased persons who possessed Social Security numbers and whose deaths have been reported to the Social Security Administration since 1962.

Surname, family, or birth name Last name at birth.

Vital records Civil records of life events (birth, marriage, death) preserved by an official source (e.g., government).

Will A legal document that explains how an individual desires his or her estate to be managed and distributed when he or she is deceased.

Bibliography

Colletta, John P. *They Came in Ships*. Provo, Utah: Ancestry, 2002.

Eichholz, Alice. *Red Book: American State, County, and Town Sources*. 3rd ed. Provo, Utah: Ancestry, 2004.

Szucs, Loretto Dennis. *They Became Americans: Finding Naturalization Records and Ethnic Origins*. Provo, Utah: Ancestry, 1998.

Szucs, Loretto Dennis, and Sandra Hargreaves Luebking. *The Source: A Guidebook to American Genealogy*. 3rd ed. Provo, Utah: Ancestry, 2006.

Szucs, Loretto Dennis, and Matthew Wright. *Finding Answers in U.S. Census Records*. Provo, Utah: Ancestry, 2002.

To order these and other Ancestry products, visit us online at <www.theancestrystore.com> or call 1-800-ANCESTRY (262-3787).

About Ancestry.com

Ancestry.com is the number one resource for family history. The website offers billions of names in thousands of databases, and new records are added to the site all the time. It is the only place online where you can find images of all the U.S. federal census schedules from 1790 to 1930. Ancestry.com offers a large variety of other records, too, including birth, marriage, death, immigration, court, and military. Many of these databases are available only through paid subscription, but some are free of charge, including the 1880 U.S. Federal Census and 1881 England and Wales Census.

Member Trees are also tremendous aids to your family history research. With hundreds of millions of names, these resources are designed to link families together through thousands of family trees submitted by researchers like yourself.

Also available is the *Ancestry Weekly Journal*, an electronic e-mail newsletter. Packed with tips, news, and updates from expert genealogists, it offers a wealth of ideas for beginners. To get your free subscription, go to Ancestry.com and click the "Learning Center" tab. Find the newsletter section and sign up!

Family historians will also find a large array of genealogical publications including the popular *Ancestry* Magazine, reference books, CDs, and other research aids, which can be ordered online at <www.the ancestrystore.com>. Check out the Ancestry.com blog, *24/7 Family History Circle* <http://blogs.ancestry.com/circle>, for updates on posted records, new resources, and anything related to family history.

Recommended Books

The following Ancestry publications are useful guides to help you take the next steps in discovering your heritage. They can be ordered online at <www.theancestrystore.com> or by calling 1-800-ANCESTRY (262-3787).

The Official Guide to Ancestry.com
by George G. Morgan
This detailed look at Ancestry.com, the #1 website for family history research, explains the site's many exciting features, helping you find your ancestors and learn their stories.

The Official Guide to RootsWeb.com
by Myra Vanderpool Gormley, CG, and Tana Pedersen Lord
Provides an insider's tour of RootsWeb.com, the world's largest, free genealogy website. Using the tips and tricks found only in this book, learn how to locate valuable research resources, connect with other users, and much more.

The Source: A Guidebook to American Genealogy, 3rd ed
edited by Loretto D. Szucs and Sandra H. Luebking
A standard reference in the field of genealogy and family history. Recipient of the "Best Reference" award from the American Library Association.

Red Book: American State, County, and Town Sources
edited by Alice Eichholz
Gives the most useful genealogical resources in each of the fifty states in the United States and the District of Columbia. Lists repositories of information in counties and towns across America.

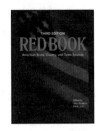

Producing a Quality Family History
by Patricia Law Hatcher
Teaches you how to create and publish your family history. It includes information on documenting facts, expressing relationships, and including illustrations of all types in your manuscript.

Printed Sources: A Guide to Published Genealogical Records
edited by Kory L. Meyerink

The most comprehensive and up-to-date directory to everything from "how-to" tutorials to "where-to" guides plus published original records, indexes, and more.

Ancestry Family Historian's Address Book: A Comprehensive List of Local, State, and Federal Agencies and Institutions and Ethnic and Genealogical Organizations
by Juliana Szucs Smith

Information on contacting national and state archives, university and public libraries, government agencies, genealogical societies, and other agencies.

They Came in Ships
by John P. Colletta

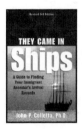

Most individuals will find at least one and, more likely, several immigrant ancestors in their family tree. The primary ports of departure and arrival are discussed as are methods for locating immigrant ancestors. Ellis Island and other immigrant stations are covered in detail.

Grandma's Memory Book

Your life is full of rich stories waiting to be told and *Grandma's Memory Book* is a way to help you share those treasured memories with the ones you love. Each page prompts you to record different parts of your life by asking thoughtful questions and providing space for you to reply.

Honoring Our Ancestors
by Megan Smolenyak Smolenyak

Fifty inspiring stories show ways that people have found to learn about and honor their ancestors. A treasure for every family historian who occasionally needs a little encouragement to carry on with the search.

Index

Worksheets and Forms

WORKSHEET A: Your Vital Information

YOUR FULL NAME _____

BIRTH Date   Place

RELIGIOUS EVENTS

Event	Date	Place

EDUCATION

	Date	Place

MARRIAGE

Spouse	Date	Place

CHILDREN

Name	Date	Place

WORKSHEET B: Your Parents' Vital Information

YOUR FATHER'S FULL NAME _____

BIRTH Date   Place

DEATH Date   Place

YOUR MOTHER'S FULL NAME _____
(first name and maiden name)

BIRTH Date   Place

DEATH Date   Place

MARRIAGE Date   Place

CHILDREN

Name	Date	Place

OTHER SIGNIFICANT EVENTS

Event	Date	Place

WORKSHEET C: Your Paternal Grandparents' Vital Information

NAME OF FATHER'S FATHER _____

BIRTH Date   Place

DEATH Date   Place

NAME OF FATHER'S MOTHER_____
(first name and maiden name)

BIRTH Date   Place

DEATH Date   Place

MARRIAGE Date   Place

CHILDREN

Name	Date	Place

OTHER SIGNIFICANT EVENTS

Event	Date	Place

WORKSHEET D: Your Maternal Grandparents' Vital Information

NAME OF MOTHER'S FATHER _____

BIRTH Date _____   Place _____

DEATH Date _____   Place _____

NAME OF MOTHER'S MOTHER _____
(first name and maiden name)

BIRTH Date _____   Place _____

DEATH Date _____   Place _____

MARRIAGE Date _____   Place _____

CHILDREN

Name	Date	Place

OTHER SIGNIFICANT EVENTS

Event	Date	Place

WORKSHEET E: Research Log

Family _____ Researcher _____

Date	Repository	Description of Source	Time Period/ Names Searched	Results
	Call #/Microfilm #			

WORKSHEET F: Contact List for Living Sources

NAME

Address

Phone

Fax

E-mail

Date of Visit

Date Letter Sent

Date Received Reply

Notes

NAME

Address

Phone

Fax

E-mail

Date of Visit

Date Letter Sent

Date Received Reply

Notes

NAME

Address

Phone

Fax

E-mail

Date of Visit

Date Letter Sent

Date Received Reply

Notes

Pedigree Chart

Chart No. _____

No. 1 on this chart is
the same person as No. _____
On Chart No. _____

1
BORN
PLACE
MARRIED
PLACE
DIED
PLACE

NAME OF SPOUSE

2
BORN
PLACE
MARRIED
PLACE
DIED
PLACE

3
BORN
PLACE
DIED
PLACE

4
BORN
PLACE
MARRIED
PLACE
DIED
PLACE

5
BORN
PLACE
DIED
PLACE

6
BORN
PLACE
MARRIED
PLACE
DIED
PLACE

7
BORN
PLACE
DIED
PLACE

8
CONT. ON CHART _____

9
CONT. ON CHART _____

10
CONT. ON CHART _____

11
CONT. ON CHART _____

12
CONT. ON CHART _____

13
CONT. ON CHART _____

14
CONT. ON CHART _____

15
CONT. ON CHART _____

http://www.ancestry.com/save/charts/ancchart.htm

Form # F120

Family Group Record

Husband Given name(s)		Last name	☐ See "Other Marriages"
Born	Place		
Christened	Place		
Died	Place		
Buried	Place		
Married	Place		
Husband's father Given name(s)		Last name	
Husband's mother Given name(s)		Maiden name	

Wife Given name(s)		Maiden name	
Born	Place		
Christened	Place		
Died	Place		
Buried	Place		
Wife's father Given name(s)		Last name	
Wife's mother Given name(s)		Maiden name	

Children   List each child in order of birth.

1	Sex	Given name(s)		Last name	☐ See "Other Marriages"
		Born	Place		
		Christened	Place		
		Died	Place		
		Spouse Given name(s)		Last name	
		Married	Place		

2	Sex	Given name(s)		Last name	☐ See "Other Marriages"
		Born	Place		
		Christened	Place		
		Died	Place		
		Spouse Given name(s)		Last name	
		Married	Place		

3	Sex	Given name(s)		Last name	☐ See "Other Marriages"
		Born	Place		
		Christened	Place		
		Died	Place		
		Spouse Given name(s)		Last name	
		Married	Place		

Prepared by	Address
Phone ( )	
Date prepared	

Family Group Record

Husband Given name(s)		Last name	☐ See "Other Marriages"
Wife Given name(s)		Maiden name	

Children   List each child in order of birth.

4	Sex	Given name(s)		Last name	☐ See "Other Marriages"
		Born	Place		
		Christened	Place		
		Died	Place		
		Spouse Given name(s)		Last name	
		Married	Place		

5	Sex	Given name(s)		Last name	☐ See "Other Marriages"
		Born	Place		
		Christened	Place		
		Died	Place		
		Spouse Given name(s)		Last name	
		Married	Place		

6	Sex	Given name(s)		Last name	☐ See "Other Marriages"
		Born	Place		
		Christened	Place		
		Died	Place		
		Spouse Given name(s)		Last name	
		Married	Place		

7	Sex	Given name(s)		Last name	☐ See "Other Marriages"
		Born	Place		
		Christened	Place		
		Died	Place		
		Spouse Given name(s)		Last name	
		Married	Place		

8	Sex	Given name(s)		Last name	☐ See "Other Marriages"
		Born	Place		
		Christened	Place		
		Died	Place		
		Spouse Given name(s)		Last name	
		Married	Place		

9	Sex	Given name(s)		Last name	☐ See "Other Marriages"
		Born	Place		
		Christened	Place		
		Died	Place		
		Spouse Given name(s)		Last name	
		Married	Place		

Family Tree Maker®

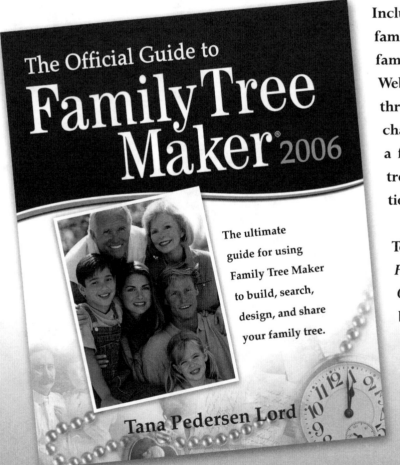

The Official Guide to Family Tree Maker® 2006

The ultimate guide for using Family Tree Maker to build, search, design, and share your family tree.

Tana Pedersen Lord

Included with this book is America's top-selling family tree software, *Family Tree Maker*. Build your family tree; search for ancestors using powerful Web search tools; and share your discoveries through books, websites, and customized tree charts. Using *Family Tree Maker*, you can create a family history that you and your family will treasure for years to come. For more information, visit <www.familytreemaker.com>.

To take advantage of all the great features that *Family Tree Maker* has to offer, you'll want *The Official Guide to Family Tree Maker*. This step-by-step guide shows you how to enter family information, design charts and reports, share your research with others, and much more. To order a guide, go to <www.theancestrystore.com> or call 1-800-ANCESTRY.

ancestrypublishing

Includes a free, 14-day trial subscription to Ancestry.com.